Blue Ghosts

poems by

Kathryn DeZur

Finishing Line Press
Georgetown, Kentucky

Blue Ghosts

Copyright © 2019 by Kathryn DeZur
ISBN 978-1-63534-968-9 First Edition
All rights reserved under International and Pan-American Copyright Conventions. No part of this book may be reproduced in any manner whatsoever without written permission from the publisher, except in the case of brief quotations embodied in critical articles and reviews.

ACKNOWLEDGMENTS

Grateful acknowledgement is made to the editors of the journals who first published the following poems. These poems were published, sometimes in a variant form, as follows:

Blueline: "Keeping Track of the Dead"
Literary Mama: A Journal for the Maternally Inclined: "Biological Determinism" and "Fibonacci Numbers." Reprint permission for "Fibonacci Numbers" was granted to *Strange Attractors: A Collection of Mathematical Love Poems*, edited by Sarah Glaz and JoAnne Growney.

Publisher: Leah Maines
Editor: Christen Kincaid
Cover Art: *Searching for Love*, Spencer Black©, Black Visual, blackvisual.com
Author Photo: Riikka Olson©
Cover Design: Elizabeth Maines McCleavy

Printed in the USA on acid-free paper.
Order online: www.finishinglinepress.com
          also available on amazon.com

Author inquiries and mail orders:
Finishing Line Press
P. O. Box 1626
Georgetown, Kentucky 40324
U. S. A.

Table of Contents

Keeping Track of the Dead 1

Matins 2

Crow 3

With Forethought of Grief 4

Miscarriage 6

The Space between Breaths 7

Moon Hunting 8

Blue Ghosts 9

Salt 10

Mosquito 11

I Cannot Give You 12

Biological Determinism 13

Fibonacci Numbers 14

Lullaby 15

Emily Dickinson Says Hope Is a Thing with Feathers 16

Bad Buddhist 17

Crustacean Dreams 18

Eels 19

Lips 20

Bad Habits 21

Chosen 22

Run 23

Resentment 24

Legend 25

Today 26

Notes 28

For Gwen and Keith

Keeping Track of the Dead

I walk the dog three times a day.
On each path, I must keep in mind
where the dead things
are: the masticated toad
near the bridge; the squirrel tail
on Cross Street; the eviscerated
rabbit on the Americorps Trail.
I must do this because the dog

likes to chew on the dead.
Once he's grabbed something, I've lost
the game—there's no way to recapture
the board-stiff remnants, other than grasping
slimy flesh and pulling. Instead,
I try to remember
where small cadavers litter side streets.

Something new dies every week or so;
he finds the bodies before I do.
I add them to the list.

I side-step my own collection of corpses—
a mother, a lover, a future with children—
carefully, eyes averted,
so they don't infect the next dream.
The pathways grow more and more crowded
with decay.

Perhaps burying them is the answer,
but that would require touching
them, and I know myself:
I would turn them over,
look in their faces,
put them in my bag,
unable to leave them behind.

Matins

The blue light of morning
is an uncertain gift,
a song sung into cold so deep
even crows elect to remain
in twiggy tree-top nests.

Head and tail lights wind
double strings of diamonds
and rubies around
the mountain's throat
as we drive to school, to work.

The light's plainsong thrums
with questions: Shall others despise
or like me today? Will Failure and Destiny dance
in space opened by a word, a glance, spilled
coffee, a dropped book? Will the crows venture
out, wait by a roadside for the happy
accident of a meal?

Crow

Harbinger of rain
eater of grasshopper eggs
thief of fire

Carrier of the sun
last of ten inky brethren
who escaped Houyi's wicked bow

Caw an omen:
visitors on the horizon—
death to enemies

A hole in my left wing
pulls you through to the otherworld
a night raven yourself

All colors absorb and dissolve
into black, all names and forms melt
into me

With Forethought of Grief

> *I go and lie down where the wood drake*
> *rests in his beauty on the water, and the great heron feeds.*
> *I come into the peace of wild things*
> *who do not tax their lives with forethought*
>   —Wendell Berry, "The Peace of Wild Things"

My mother, my marriage, my unborn child,
my sense of safety—all dead,
my thoughts turn
to the future, a daughter
distressed or just gone
the way that children go, the ache
that remains in their place.
It is only one future, I know,
and before I break
I go and lie down where the wood drake

swims, the water's warm buoyancy
promising to carry, lift my prone form,
but still I cannot trust.
My legs kick and arms flail—
they must do something, anything
to keep from sinking, down where reeds
rot and fish hide,
uncomfortable even in shallows
where the swan breeds,
rests in his beauty on the water, and the great heron feeds.

I try again, breathe
air mixed with moss
and dew, yellow leaves falling,
green leaves still,
water carving holes in granite.
The fox, avoiding the trap, brings
a dead shrew to its den.

I try to believe that
where the swan flaps his great white wings,
I come into the peace of wild things.

This is what I long
for: placid
water, wood drake swimming,
great heron feeding, fox sliding
through brush on delicate black paws,
sunshine caught
on ochre leaves; to survive
only today's sorrow, to live like wild
things, who do not suffer grief's unyielding knot,
who do not tax their lives with forethought.

Miscarriage

What starts as a cloud—
expansive,
ethereal—condenses
to a bloody stone,
drops soundless
through muddied
water, settles
on creek bed, solid,
immovable.

The Space between Breaths

i.
The doe dips
her head to fallen
apples, nibbles
around their sweet
brown rot.

ii.
White-bearded fox,
sly as a whistle,
crouches low in devil's grass,
scrutinizes the chicken coop.

iii.
The crow grasps the worm—
hatchlings croak their desire,
beaks gape,
sooty feathers shiver.

iv.
Wings like leaded
glass flex,
emerald body
contracts, lays eggs
in decay.

Moon Hunting

New moon
on its knees.

Sickle's crescent slices
words from sounds, words
from meaning.

Sky tides pull silicon sand,
push against gain, against
loss.

Full moon drawn taut, double bows
strung with contrary desires.

Blue Ghosts

Blue ghosts hover and hum low,
sizzle and spark with arctic fire
luminous against night's shadow.
Blue ghosts hover and hum low,
transparent bodies' phosphorescent glow
darts between scarlet oak and bull briar.
Blue ghosts hover and hum low,
sizzle and spark with arctic fire.

Salt

Mix white sorrow
with my ashes,
pinch then toss
white hope
over both shoulders
so I do not follow
you home, eternally
hungry
for the tang
of Earth and Sea
on my tongue.

Mosquito

Needle
sharp as envy—
you never even feel
it enter.

I Cannot Give You

I cannot give you everything—

I cannot give
the tangled piece
of horsehair,
leather, bleached bone,
sandstone—

despite the small perfect starfish
of your mouth, the translucent shell
of your ear.

Biological Determinism

I curled into an orange plastic chair, scabby
knees to bony chest, coiled
against antiseptic smells and squeaking
soles of nurses' shoes rubbing
on gray linoleum. Across the hall,
my mother lay dying.
A young doctor, white coat flapping,
paused, studied me clinically.
"Are you comfortable like that?"
he asked. When my head bobbed,
he gave a sharp nod of his own. "It's the fetal
position. How you were in the womb,"
he said, and moved briskly
on. My first lover

complained: "I can't hold
you when you lie there like that."
I tightened my body
further until he abandoned
the bed. Now, years later,

I curl around my burgeoning
belly. The cat sleeps draped
around me, connecting knees
and breasts that no longer meet,
her dark fur a comma
between security and the rest.

Fibonacci Numbers

At a hard wood desk, on a hard
wooden stool, a mathematician counted rings
of monastery bells next door, seeking
God in multiplying numbers. He considered the problem
of ideal fertility: rabbits in fields of buttercups,
daisies, asters, chicory, reproducing at the rate of one
pair per month. The arithmetical series revealed a mean, a golden
number, controlling the growth of leaves, pinecones
tossed in the fire cold winter nights, cauliflower he despised, seeds
that taunted Eve when she delved into the apple
seeking knowledge and gaining children.

I, too, chant the count of hope
each night: one ovum. One sperm. Two eyes. Three
letter names—Ann or Ian. Five fingers per hand. A perfect
nautilus spiral of an ear. I long for the fertility
of Fibonacci's numbers, that mystical statistical world
where one plus one equals three.

Lullaby

Smell of oncoming snow
murmurs long and low

Exhausted phlox nod,
whisper sepia sighs

Crows croon warning,
Caution! Caution! Caution!

Scythe and shovel rock and sing
as I put the garden to bed.

Emily Dickinson Says Hope Is a Thing with Feathers

If it is,
it's an emu,
flightless and awkward,
drab brown feathers dragging
across its back,
beautiful only
at its beginning, a teal egg
bigger than two hands
can cup.
This emu's heart
thumps slowly—
nothing like the ruby-throated
hummingbird who flits
and flitters,
who has a humming heart
that beats beats beats
four times faster.
But the emu's pulse quickens
when she considers
what it would feel like
to be the clever crow,
glossy black feathers
and screeching caws,
or the chickadee
seeking seeds in snow,
the nightingale mesmerizing
mates with its song. The emu's pulse
quickens as she longs to become
anything, anything
that can fly.

Bad Buddhist

Desire
has seated herself
in my chair, at my desk,
presses my pen
against pursed lips
as she dreams
of what she wants:

Sunshine and cool breezes,
clouds and rain every tenth day.
Swinging on swing sets,
feet touching sky,
descent controlled.
Every good moment
of my daughter's growing
up—*Good Night Moon*
and pinecone art and
more than one imaginary
world open at a time.
None of the bad—
105° fevers and terror
after the divorce
that I no longer resemble
her mother and lost
fairies, no longer guarding
her childhood bedroom.
Friends who stay
and trees that don't fall,
but still all the good
that comes from friends leaving
and trees falling.

Over and over,
I hand her the pen,
invite her to sit in my chair.

Crustacean Dreams

What do lobsters dream,
gazing through the flat glass
of supermarket holding tanks?
Of glorious battles, pincers snapping,
claws unbound by rubber?
Schools of silvery fish darting
in unilateral rhythm, an easy
meal for the taking? Murky
water and slow walks along beachy
sand? Or, do they dream

of cruising with sharks,
controlling ocean
currents, skimming surfaces
on jet skis? Parasailing
beneath pale blue skies? Certainly not

the pot, the boiling water, the scream,
a clean white plate and clarified
butter. Surely never of becoming
so deliciously sweet,
dreams tucked deep
in their now red shells, now
opaque flesh.

Eels
>*for Carol*

Eels carry a history
of transparency,
once glass filaments
floating among tangled
tan branches, pale berries.
For a time, they stretch
small and sinuous,
color of kelp
or lost Spanish treasure,
slide along mud
and gravel.
Finally caught,
soon to become
a family meal, they bear
beneath dull silver skin
the flashing turquoise
of a boundless
Sargasso Sea.

Lips

What lips my lips have kissed, and where, and why,
I cannot remember them all—so many lips,
lips hard as saddle leather, passive as fish,
wintertime lips, snow crystals warming
their edges. I have savored festival lips
in carnival colors, plum-blossom lips, drowsy
lips just roused from sleep. I've bitten
my lip, given lip service to love, read
foreign lips by Braille. Some incandescent
kisses sparkled like liparite, dense
and clear, while lipless kisses left
me indifferent, my own lips stiff and resistant.
But your lips, still untasted, full and clever,
Those lips, my darling, will I remember forever.

Bad Habits

Not like chasing fireflies
just after dusk,
small malachite lights
dancing slowly
across dark grass
blinking mythic
patterns—
catch me if you can.

Not like that.

The burning light,
spotted dun wings
fluttering quickly,
silently.

Chosen

She crawls beneath
the comforter, stretches
next to my husband's sleeping
body. She rides beside
me in the car, slides
up as I walk from the library,
slips past my office door, sets
flies buzzing and rattling
against the windows. She stands
before me, pale face gazing
into mine like a lover, ragged wings
furled. She digs her talons
deep into my abdomen, whispers—
I am Pain
and you
have been Chosen.

Run

That moment. You
know the one. That moment

when you think
Shit. What have I done?
When your stepmother,
second weekday Manhattan
on her breath, snatches
up the ceramic wastebasket,
preparing to hurl it
at your father's head,
and you step between
them. When your boyfriend

tells you he loves
you, but you shouldn't wear
that top, you must want
men to stare at your breasts,
and besides, you don't know
how good you've got
it. At those moments, child,

remember. Remember
the paths open in front
of you, shady lanes, dusty
gravel, steaming tarmac.
Remember that God

gave you legs
for a reason.

Resentment

Barnacles seek seams
where rivets puncture
steel, search out scars
caused by scraping

against rock.
Their bone eyes open
only at feeding time,
their cemented colonies
lava flows of stone.
Even when dead,

they leave fossilized
empty centers
inviting further settlement.

Legend

Ravens hatch white,
subsist on dew,
consume clouds
in reflected heavens,
drop
by
drop.

Today

> *The world goes on as it must,*
> *The bees in the garden rumbling a little,*
> *The fish leaping, the gnats getting eaten.*
> *And so forth.*
> —Mary Oliver, "Today"

Today is filled with tasks—tasks
that must be done, should be done,
will or won't or can't be done:
teach, launder, cook, dust,
resurrect calla lily bulbs
now soft and spotted with rot,
stretch two dimes into seven,
soothe the teething baby, write
a poem, build scaffolds of trust.
The world goes on as it must.

In the farmer's field across the way,
some lost Greek goddess sowed lions' teeth
whose tap roots now reach
down to nourish yellow pistils
with magma and fire.
My daughter gathers fistfuls of clouds,
blows her fragmented wishes
across our yard, each bit destined
to root a new wish, sustenance for the beetles,
the bees in the garden rumbling a little.

On my morning drive, mist lays like lace gloves
in valleys. A pungent black and white carcass
inspires a crow's greedy hops,
dame's spear stands at attention, glistens
with dew. Horses in meadows crop
grass, whip tails, swat gadflies.
Around a bend appears a lake, color
of gulls' wings, tight waves slapping
the dock; I can almost hear them if I listen,
the fish leaping, the gnats getting eaten.

Daisies adorn the dining room table.
My husband's hands fold clothes, wash
dishes, touch my hair, my face.
He reads Wordsworth
in bed, book resting against cream sheets,
light glinting off his wedding ring.
The rhythm of marriage
takes over, sparks then soothes
today's annoyances, this home, this hearth,
and so forth.

Notes

"With Forethought of Grief" and "Today" are poems in the *glosa* form, which begins with four lines drawn from another poem; each of these becomes the final line of four ten-line stanzas. Within each stanza, lines 4, 9, and 10 rhyme.

"Blue Ghosts" was inspired by Spencer Black's photograph of blue ghost fireflies, *Searching for Love*, which is the cover art for this collection.

"Lips" is a sonnenizio, a sonnet form created by poet Kim Addonizio, in which the first line comes from another sonnet, and one word from that line must be repeated in each subsequent line. The final two lines form a couplet. The first line here is drawn from Edna St. Vincent Millay's "What Lips My Lips Have Kissed, and Where, and Why (Sonnet XLIII)."

"Legend" was inspired by a medieval theory that ravens were born white and survived on dew until they turned black. My thanks to Archie Cornish for introducing me to this strange bit of natural history.

Additional Acknowledgments

Many thanks to Leah Maines for choosing this manuscript. There are many who have been crucial partners in the revision process, including the Delhi Women Poets (Sharon Ruetenik, Carol Little, Arlene Metrick, Sandra Russell, Kenna Levendosky, Laura Pierson, and Sharon Cucinado Israel), who have workshopped poems faithfully every two weeks for many years. Richard Levine provided suggestions on "Matins," making it a much better poem. A special thank you goes to Lynn Domina, who has read and commented on every one of my poems for 20 years. And of course, thanks are due to my always-first and best readers, Gwen Hilson and Keith Humphreys, for their suggestions, their love, and their unending support.

Kathryn DeZur teaches writing and literature at the State University of New York College of Technology at Delhi. Her poems have appeared in *Blueline, The Fourth River, Fickle Muses, Literary Mama, The Teacher's Voice, Mother Verse,* and *Women's Studies,* as well as in anthologies such as *Strange Attractors: A Collection of Mathematical Love Poems* and *Zeus Seduces the Wicked Stepmother in the Saloon of the Gingerbread House.* Her academic specialty is medieval and Renaissance English literature. She is the recipient of both the SUNY Chancellor's Award for Excellence in Teaching (2010) and the SUNY Chancellor's Award for Excellence in Scholarship and Creative Activity (2016). She has lived in the northern reaches of the Catskill Mountains for twenty years, having moved there from California. She resides in a small college town with her daughter Gwen and husband Keith.

www.ingramcontent.com/pod-product-compliance
Ingram Content Group UK Ltd.
Pitfield, Milton Keynes, MK11 3LW, UK
UKHW041303180426
11947UKWH00009B/644